FIST OF FURY VOL 1

Photo Collection

"Fist of Fury The Chinese Connection Vol. 1", by Rick Baker
Compiled by Rick Baker. Foreword by Rick Baker
Contributors: Andrew Staton, Charles Damiano, Johnny Burnett,
Michael Nesbitt, James Mckeon, GLynn Darbyshire, Thomas Gross
Cover design: Tim Hollingsworth
Photographs from the EH Archives

Design & Layout, Nic Cairns, 22:22 Creative Media

Special thanks to: K.Reeve, George Tan, Ting Wai Ho, Nic Cairns,
Nick Singh, Alan Donkin, Brett Ratner.
Additional research material Wikipedia, *South Morning China Post*
Special mention to my mum who was as big a kung fu movie fans as me.
Special thanks to Sylvester (Sly) Raymond for being a good friend.

Special dedication to Chan Yuk. Thank you for the many images and moments in time you
left, of one of the greatest icons the world has even known – BRUCE LEE, 1940 – 1973

Every effort to trace the copyright holders of the illustrations and original layouts in this book.
In the event that any have been inadvertently overlooked, please contact the publishers
so that the situation can be rectified in future editions.

Please note: The photographs within these pages have been presented in their best quality format. Some original negatives had slight damage and it was decided to leave them as seen for authenticity (sometimes over exposed and slighty out of focus). Some contact sheets had light scratches due to age. Printing on a matt paper can sometimes highlight these issues, but time and care has been taken with the images used to give the reader the best quality presentation.

First published by Eastern Heroes © 2021. All Rights Reserved.
www.easternheroes.com
FIRST EDITION

ISBN: 978-1-7398519-3-4

All rights reserved. No parts of this publication may be reproduced or transmitted in any
form or by any means, graphic, electronic or mechanical, including photocopying, recording,
taping or any information storage and retrieval system, without prior written permission of the publisher.

OTHER TITLES AVAILABLE

Amazon.com • Barnes & Noble • Blackwells.co.uk • easternheroes.com

FIST OF FURY

Release date 22 March 1972 (Hong Kong)

"In the beginning the world had only flirted with martial art movies.
It was not until Bruce Lee came along that the world fell in love with them."

INTRODUCTION
RICK BAKER

I decided a few months ago to get in touch with some old school Bruce lee connoisseur collectors and ask them the impact that Bruce Lee's *Fist of Fury* had when they first saw it at the cinema. A lot of today's newer audience would have discovered Bruce lee through Video, TV or in some case DVD.

The Bruce lee films have aged well and are constantly being reissued as quality upgrades from DVD to 1080p 2K and more recently 4K.

Fist of Fury was the third Bruce lee movie I saw, my first being *The Big Boss* and then *Enter the Dragon*, both in 1974. I had been turned away numerous times by my local cinema in Hinckley but my persistence and disguises had paid dividends after many failed attempts and finally opting to use the Fleapit cinema in Earl Shilton where the ticket desk was manned by an elderly lady who had apparently, (rumour had it) that she let kids from my school into X certificates in their school uniform. But in 1975 I was fifteen but still baby-faced. I managed to get an older looking friend to purchase tickets for the Hinckley screening and for whatever reason the gods smiled and pushing my way through the crowded foyer looking towards the ground I found myself sitting near the front awaiting to see Bruce Lee once again on the big screen.

By now I had reached fever pitch as a Bruce Lee fan, collecting what magazines and *Kung Fu Monthly* that were available at the time and looking eagerly at the photos from *Fist of Fury*. What made this film exciting was that by now the word nunchaku had swept the movie going world. We had all made a set and attempted to use them poorly.

Rare photo of the Flea pit in Earl Shilton

The now closed Hinckley Classic cinema where i saw most of my kung fu films

Fist of Fury was going to see Bruce use not one, but two sets of nunchakus and at that point in my life to see him twirl those singing rods of iron simultaneously was worth the price of the 50p ticket alone.

Luckily for me the censorship of the nunchakus had not yet reached the hierarchy of the BBFC at that point which effected later the screening of both *Way of the Dragon* and *G.O.D.*

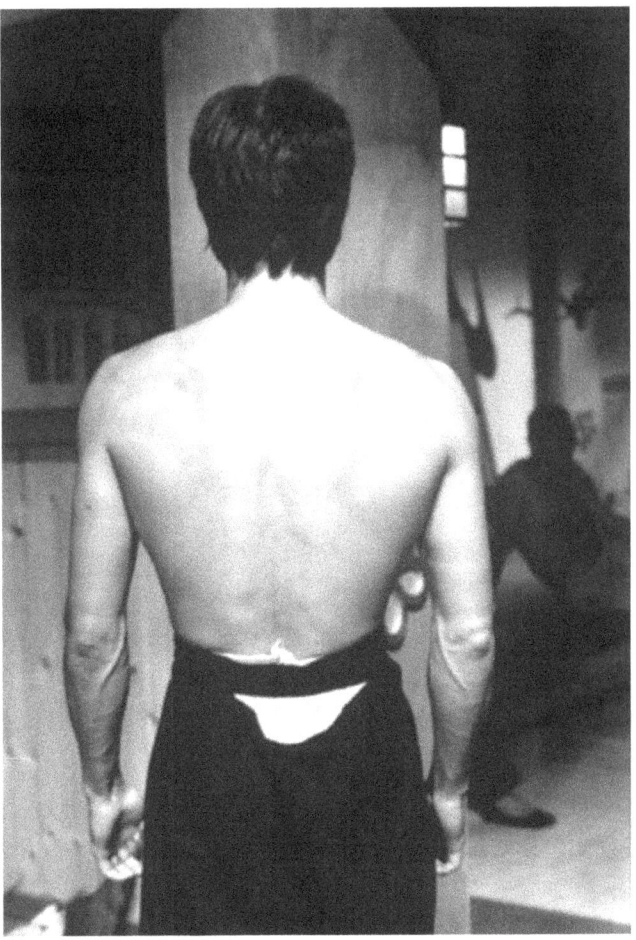

This was to be Bruce's second movie, his on screen charisma and fight action was boosted in my thoughts by the success of The Big Boss. He was clearly in charge delivering a performance that had the normally quite audience clapping and cheering. Personally I find it hard to say my favourite Bruce Lee film but I think at a push I would if I could only take one to a desert island it would be Fist of Fury.

Over the years we have become much more knowledgeable on Bruce Lee and his input and behind the scenes involvement. Steve Kerridge's Intercepting Fist revealed much information bringing even the novice on this movie up to expert standard. In this issue we really take the point of view from the fans and their many years of supporting and dedication to collecting what can only be described as priceless collections due to the memories they hold.

Please enjoy both volumes and a special thank you to those that contributed both with stories and photos from their private collections highlighting some very rare pieces of Fist of Fury memorabilia.

Facts of Fury

- Because of the movie's racial content and personal disagreements, Bruce Lee quit working with writer and Director Lo Wei after this movie.

- Jackie Chan doubled for Chikara Hashimoto for the scene where Chen kicks him out of the window. He took the kick and flew several feet. Bruce Lee immediately checked to see if he was okay. Chan later played a guard Lee kills in Enter The Dragon (1973).

- Bruce Lee openly admitted that in real-life, nunchaku versus the katana was actually an uneven match and should be avoided.

- While filming in a park, writer and Director Lo Wei had to contend with local street gangs, whose leaders would demand payment for using 'their bit' of the road. The protection money was usually paid, much to the annoyance of Bruce Lee, who had to be physically restrained from attacking them.

- According to certain historical sources in China, the real-life Chen escaped from Shanghai successfully.

- In the movie, Chen Zhen sets out to avenge the death of his teacher, Huo Yuanjia. At one point, the Chinese Wushu students are called "sick men of Asia" by their rivals. In real-life, Huo Yuanjia was a legendary Wushu martial artist. In 1901, he accepted the challenge of a Russian fighter who called Chinese people "sick men of Asia."

- Sync sound was not widely used in Hong Kong cinema for a long time. The voices were dubbed even on the original Cantonese track.

- Robert Baker (Petrov) was a student and friend of Bruce Lee's (Chen Zhen), and was recommended for the role by Lee.

- Much of the budget was spent on creating the two Japanese buildings and gardens with bridges and pools.

- This was the first film where Bruce Lee wielded his famous nunchucks, although he had previously used them in The Green Hornet (1966). It was also their first use on film.

6 Fist of Fury Photographic Collection Vol. 1

Fist of Fury Photographic Collection Vol. 1

- The international title was *Fist of Fury*. In the United States, the English dubbed version was released as *The Chinese Connection* to avoid confusion with *Fists of Fury*, the title for the U.S. release of Bruce Lee's previous movie, *The Big Boss* (1971). The U.S. title was a play on the title of the highly popular movie, *The French Connection* (1971).

- According to the book *I Am Jackie Chan: My Life in Action*, Chan observed an argument on the set between Lee and director Lo Wei. When it looked like the fight would get physical, Lo hid behind his wife, Liu Liang-hua. She was eventually able to calm Lee down.

- As with *The Big Boss* (1971), improbable stunts were added at Writer and Director Lo Wei's insistence, such as Bruce Lee lifting up a rickshaw.

- Filming was completed in six weeks.

- In 2021 *Fist of Fury* became became the first feature film to be dubbed into an Australian language, and screened in Australia as *Fist of Fury Noongar Daa*. Noongar language is the original language from the area now called the south west of Western Australia, and is now endangered. The new Noongar dialogue was based on the film's original Cantonese dialogue and new English subtitles were created to best represent the Noongar dialogue.

- Short music cues composed for the score from *Flight of the Doves* (1971) by Roy Budd are heard throughout this film.

- The death by poisoning of Bruce Lee's character's master Ho Yuan-chia serves as the premise for this movie. Jet Li's *Fearless* (2006) offers another version of how Ho Yuan-chia was poisoned.

- At the 17 minute mark when the Japanese student approaches Bruce Lee in the dojo (training gym), the hakama (traditional Japanese pants) he is wearing are on backwards.

- To make the point that crime and violence don't pay, Bruce Lee insisted that his character must die at the end, but die with honour.

- About midway through the movie, Fan, the eldest student, reveals to the other students that Feng and Tien poisoned their Teacher. The actor who plays Fan is credited as Feng Tien.

- Contrary to rumours, Steve Martin does not play the white-haired policeman who shoots Lee at the end of the movie. Hong Kong movie expert Bey Logan originated the rumour with a tongue-in-cheek remark in his commentary for the DVD issued by Hong Kong Legends (HKL). Logan apologised and retracted the remark in a later commentary recorded for HKL's re-issue of the DVD.

Fist of Fury Photographic Collection Vol. 1

HOW BRUCE ROCKED ENGLAND
ANDREW STATON – MARTIAL ARTS ILLUSTRATED

After mid-February 1974 and the explosion of *Enter The Dragon* to the British public, not only was there a craze to learn and understand everything about martial arts but there was an immediate craving for Bruce Lee in action on the big screen. As we know, due to his untimely death, all he left us was three Chinese films made in Hong Kong and made solely for the Asian market place. This meant that the context of the film was not made with western audiences in mind. However, the producers of the movies, Golden Harvest Films and its managing director Raymond Chow thought that because there was such a desperate need for people who wanted to see anything Bruce then it was worth releasing these films to a non-Asian audience.

When *Fist Of Fury* was released in the UK it was nearly totally uncut. As we all know now the film deals with topics of injustice, grief, revenge and consequences. In fact, when I first saw Bruce playing Chen Zhen he seemed to go through extreme grief after the death of his teacher (Sifu). So much so that he gets bashed on the head by his superior because he is acting so fanatical at the funeral, by falling on his master's grave and trying to dig him up. To a westerner it seemed very strange for such an outburst but later when you understand Chinese martial arts culture the sifu sometimes is closer family than their real family.

As the movie unfolds, I saw that the grief was eating away at Zhen as well as the injustice he and his peers feel from the Japanese racism towards them. The film all-in-all shows Zhen going all-out to get revenge; however the cost is dear, losing the majority of his peers and his freedom at the end.

Upon its release in the north of England there was several things that were strange to me, not that it impaired the action of the movie or its content, just things that I had not seen or accepted in western films. Firstly, was the voice dubbing, it was quite strange to see Chinese actors with American gangster voices i.e., "How can a healthy man die" or "You must be tired of living". But the need to see Bruce in action outweighed the strangeness of the dialogue, and over time became the norm even though it was not Bruce's real voice.

The second strange thing was that the film would go in and out of focus, something these days the audience would not put up with when every person and their dogs have camera phones with extreme high quality; however, in 1974 we were happy with anything saying Bruce Lee on it including clones.

I am pleased to say when Hong Kong Legends released the films uncut back in the early 2000s – this was illuminated in all of the original Bruce Lee films.

One thing that really hit you was Bruce's fantastic speed in punching and kicking which looked magnificent on film; also when it came to the signature Nunchaku fight dealing with multiple attackers, the action was just jaw dropping. This, mixed with Bruce's charisma and charm, plus his unique acting style of sinister glances and clenched fists, and the classic Chinese thumb wiping of the nose, which he interjected whilst keeping the action going

through a series of furious kung fu fights the likes that had never been seen by a western audience before. Towards the end of the movie the audience and I were all moved in a anti-Japanese direction and that China was not the "Sick Man Of Asia" as said to the kung fu school earlier in the movie. All thanks to one American/Chinese man, Bruce Lee.

Over time I went to see *Fist of Fury* at the cinema more times than I can remember as videos were very much in their infancy. It was strange to see changes to the film over time, firstly the nunchaku scene was totally removed from both times it appeared in the film. Then other violent action scenes were cut so much so that if the local newspaper the *Yorkshire Evening Post* actually advertised when *Fist of Fury* was showing, that the film was an abridged version; this was because the cinema management were constantly asked if it was a cut version of the film. I therefore presume, that having this knowledge fans just did not bother going to see that version. Also, then later on the opening credits were changed and then put back into the movie – for the first time saw Chen Zhen eating the small roasted animal, showing that the censorship council were constantly bombarded with requests to let Bruce's films to be shown uncut. All in all, it's a terrific film, so much so that the story has been told many times in Chinese film with different actors, but never really capturing the power that Bruce delivered on the big screen.

My final thought on this fantastic movie is not the movie itself but the experience I had at a showing at the Tower Cinema, Upper Briggate, Leeds. Towards the end of the movie, when Chen Zhen climbs into the first floor of his kung fu school and sees the devastation caused by the Japanese visit he hits his fist into his hand. At this point a witty guy sitting behind me spurted out "Shucks Batman" as this was the same gesture Robin did in the 1960s *Batman* TV series. Of course it brought a smile to my face as Bruce had fought Burt Ward (Robin) in the *Batman* episode *Batman's satisfaction*. From that day I always wondered if Bruce had used that expressive movement he learnt from his friend and short-time martial arts student Burt. I will leave you with that thought on my memories of what has to be one of Mr Lee's best legacy movies.

Fist of Fury Photographic Collection Vol. 1

PUBLICITY SHOTS

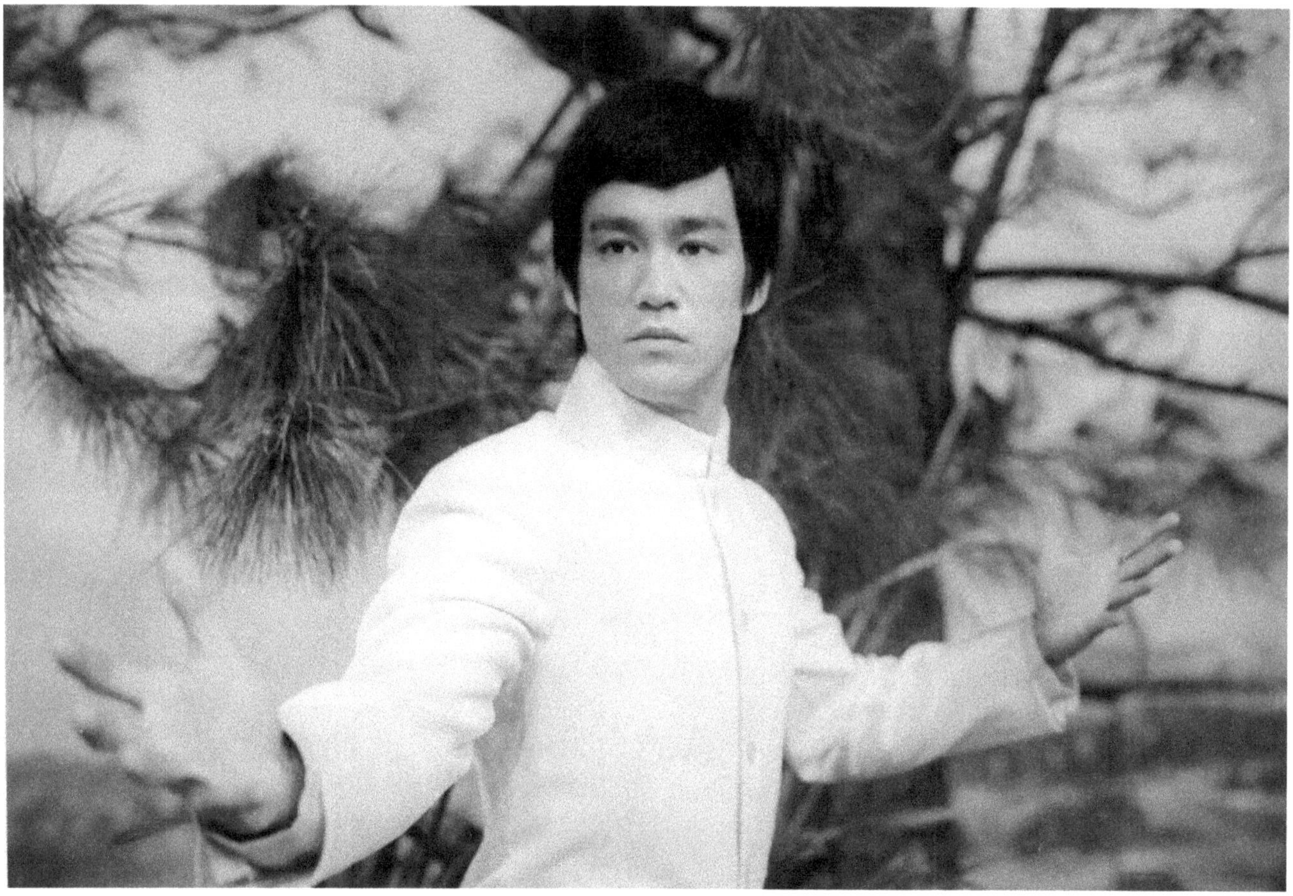

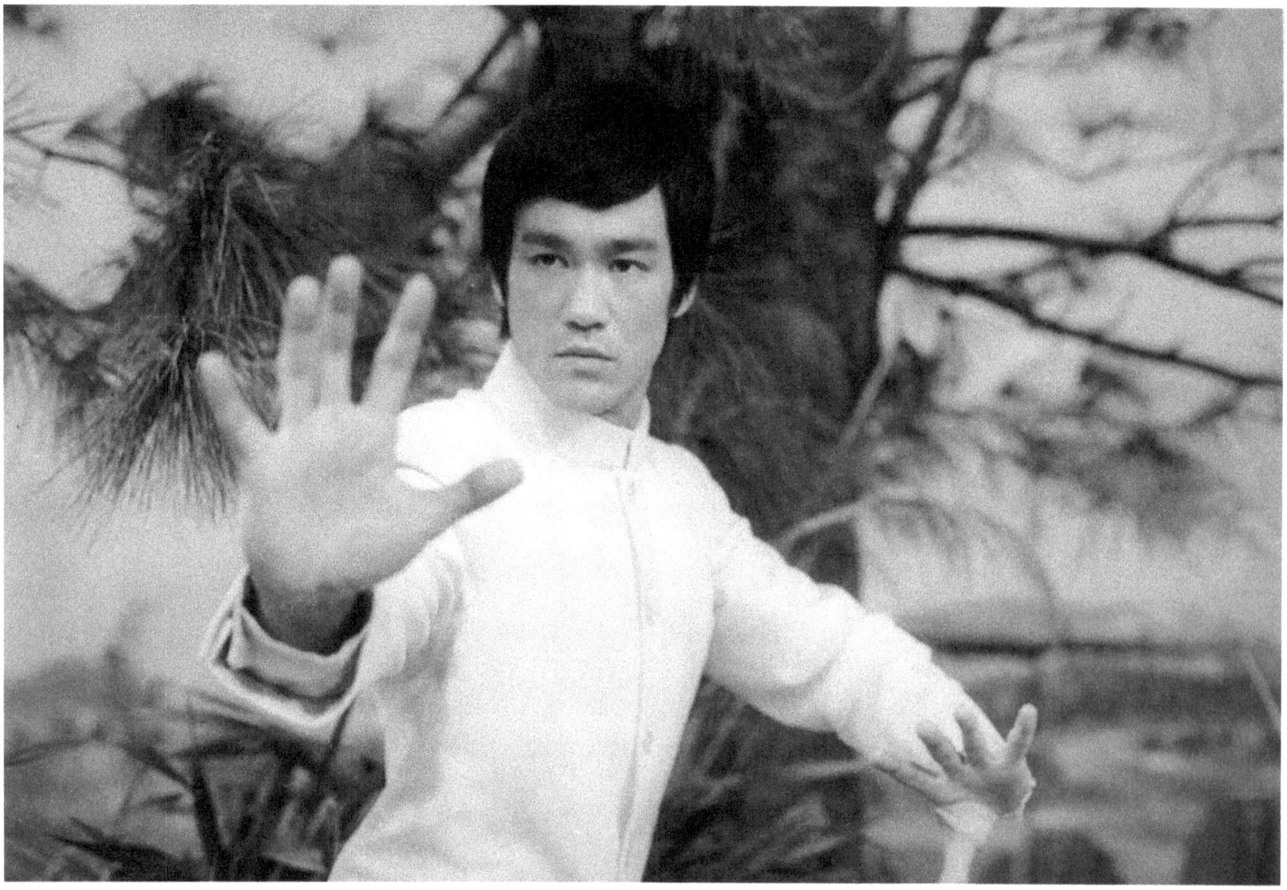

Fist of Fury Photographic Collection Vol. 1

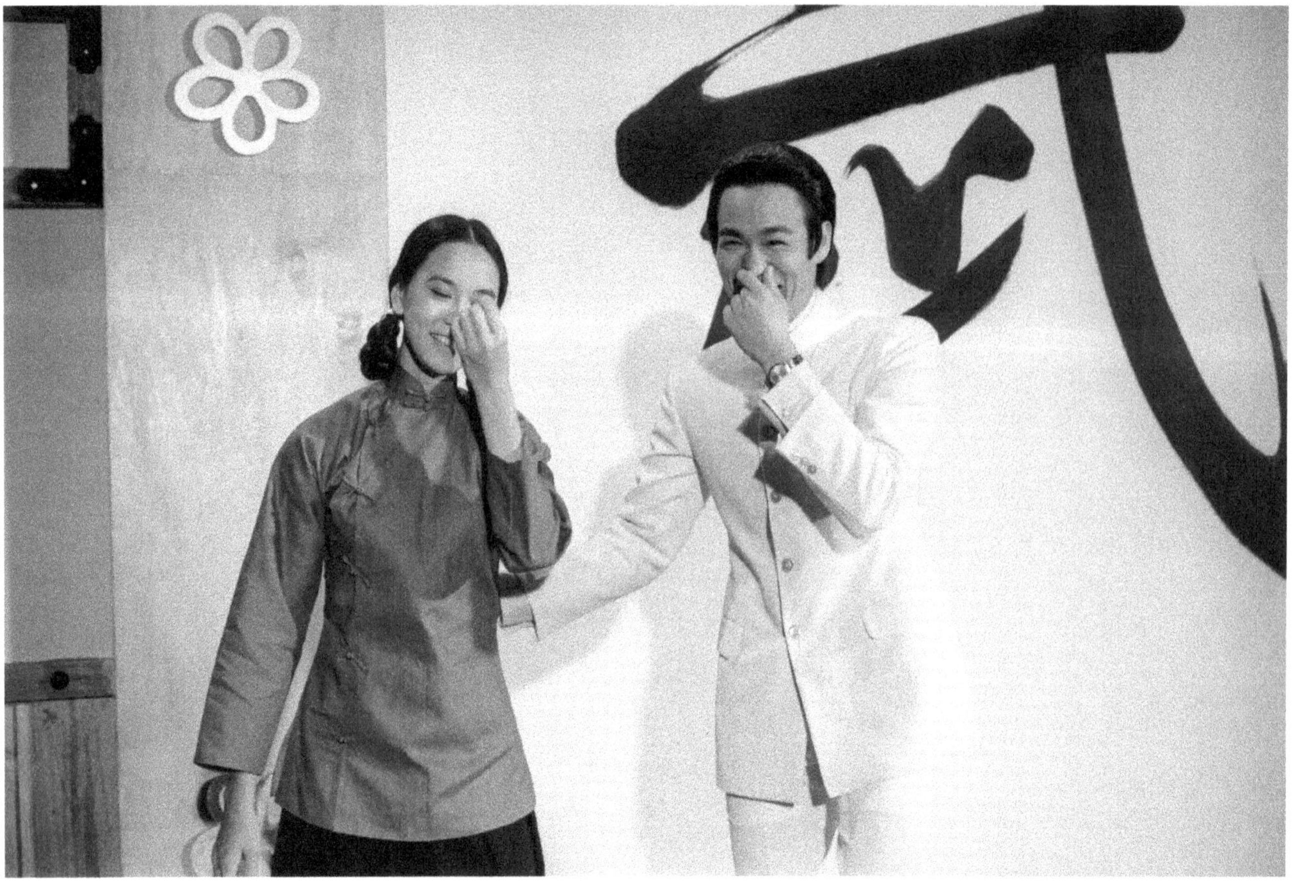

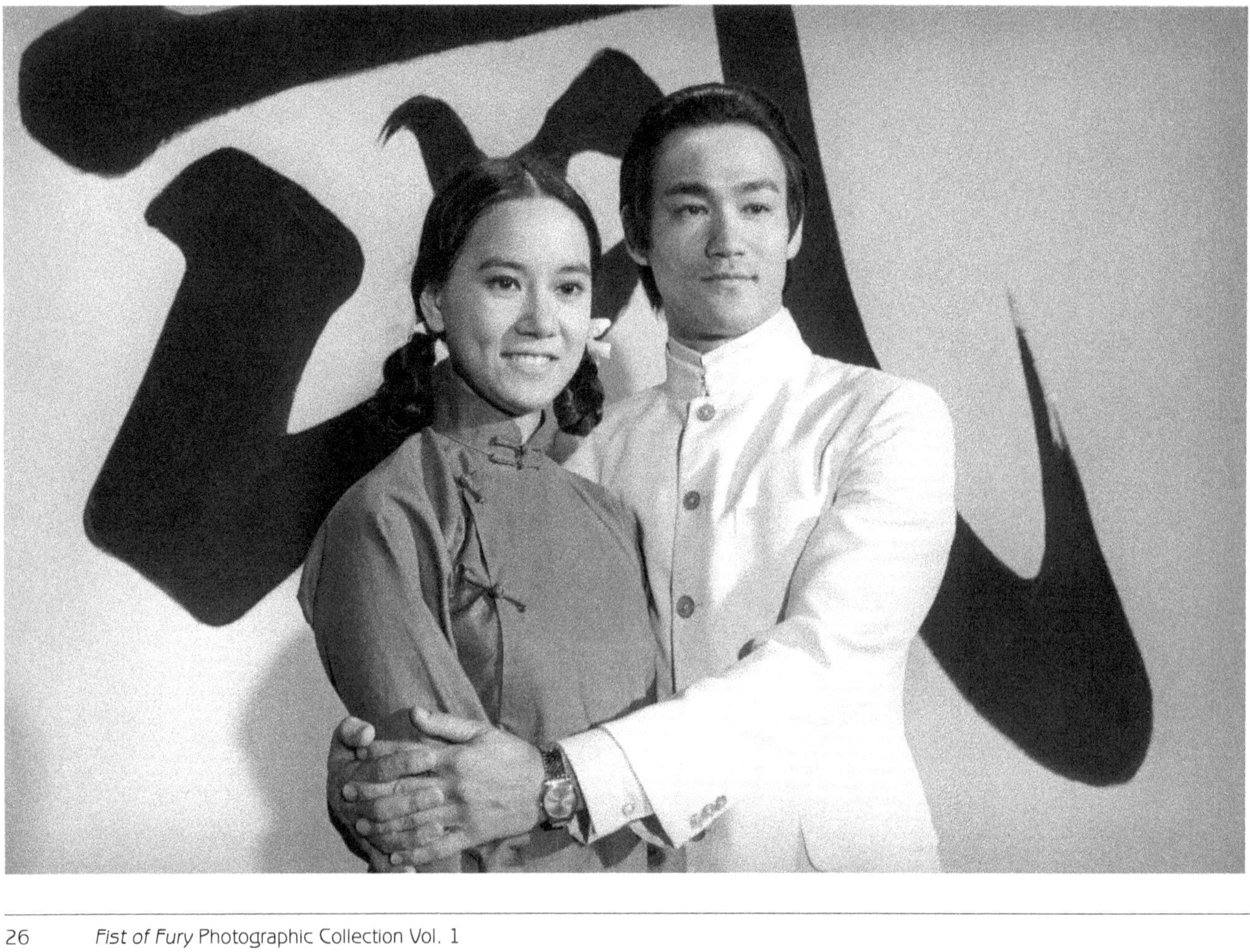

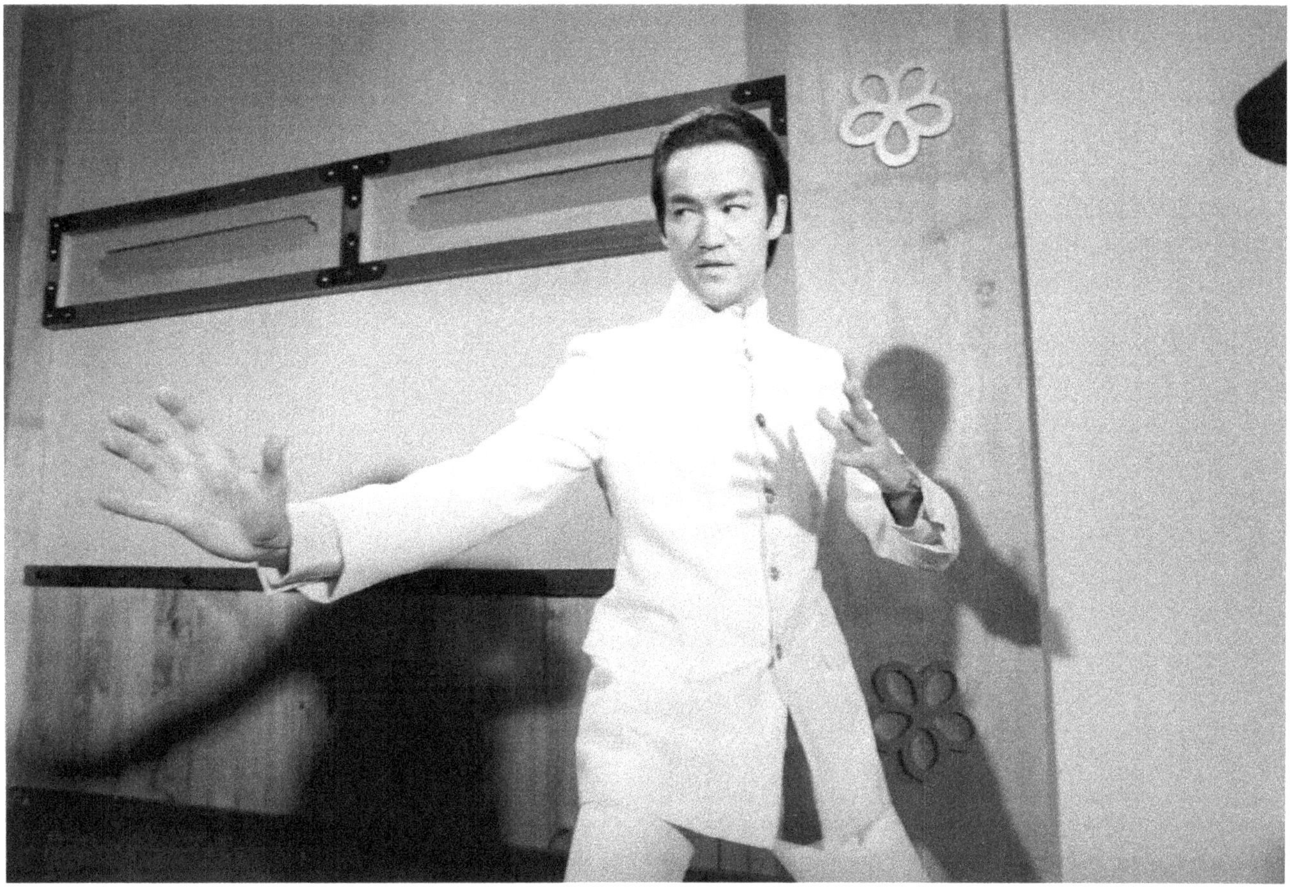

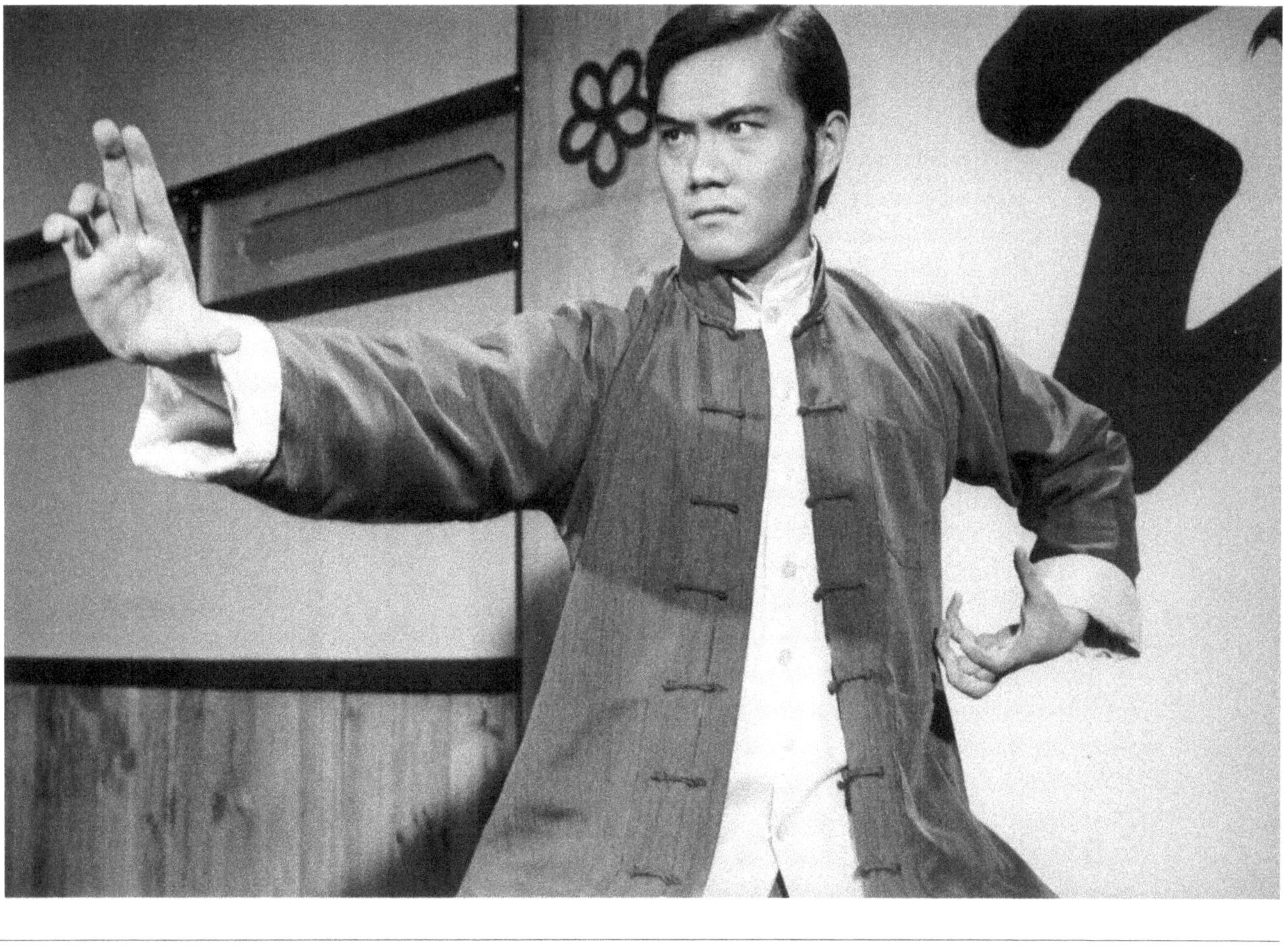

THE CHARLES DAMIANO CONNECTION

I have been a Bruce Lee fan and collector of Bruce Lee collectibles since 1973, when first seeing Bruce Lee explode off the screen in *Fists of Fury*, back in New York City's Jefferson Theater on 14th Street and 3rd Avenue! Although I was intrigued by him in 1966/67 playing Kato on *The Green Hornet* – being only eight years old at the time, my passion, fascination and intense interest in him, began in 1973!

Why Bruce Lee's *Chinese Connection*, as it was called in the United States upon its release 1973, took me to TOTAL OBSESSION for the Man is pretty obvious to most Bruce Lee fans! At that time Bruce Lee was like nothing anyone as seen before and in *Chinese Connection* he upped his level of SKILL, ON SCREEN PRESENSE, PERSONALITY and FURY by ten fold! This film is a classic but then all of Bruce's completed films are classics! This is an intensely gritty kung fu film unlike Bruce's later films which were more escapist in nature and *Chinese Connection* has the highest body count in terms of Bruce actually killing people with his fists and feet! The legendary 'Sick Man Of Asia' scene is amazing and took me over the top after seeing him take on the entire Japanese school! This fight scene even is among the greatest ever filmed since the choreography and timing is totally incredible, as the one take lasts very long without edits, and Bruce Lee kicks and hits about a dozen Japanese victims during that scene and the timing and stunt men had to be totally on point! Man just AMAZING!

He also introduces us to the nunchaku for the FIRST TIME to help him take on the entire Japanese school! My passion and excitement for this scene at fourteen years old was mind blowing! And then defeating the Japanese head instructor as well, using cat-like speed and sounds simply blew me away!

On the other hand, this film is really beautiful as it depicts the sensitive love between Bruce and Nora Mao, who is very beautiful and sweet in this film. The scene at the teacher's grave is one of the most intense and sensitive scenes of love I've ever seen. The themes in this film are mainly about relationships between individuals and humans in general, so the film has many things to offer more than mere action. This is an action classic with heart!

Bruce Lee was just INCREDIBLE in *Chinese Connection*, and his martial art skills were PHENOMENAL! What also amazed me was the climactic duels with the Russian boxer, Petrov, played by Bruce Lee personal friend Bob Baker – which has to be one of my favourite one-on-one

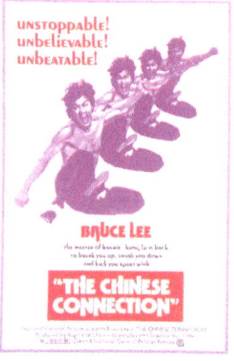

30   *Fist of Fury* Photographic Collection Vol. 1

fights of all time! And the battle with Suzuki, Chief Teach and Japanese swordsman, and the FURY he radiates when kicking him through the door at the end of the film is powerful and classic!

This is the best movie Bruce Lee has made before starring in *Enter The Dragon*, and if you're a Bruce Lee fan please watch this movie, you'll just love it!

Charles Damiano, Bruce Lee Collector and Fan
Founder of Charles Damiano's Bruce Lee Collection YouTube Channel
YouTube Channel: https://www.youtube.com/user/charlesdamiano/featured
Website: www.BruceLeeCollection.com

vol 2

FIST OF FURY
JOHNNY 'FANATICAL DRAGON' BURNETT

Simply put... *Fist of Fury* is Bruce Lee's greatest film. Whilst it may not be every fan's favourite, it's hard to find another film in Bruce Lee's tragically short filmography that packs as much punch in terms of its cinematic legacy. The enduring appeal of the character Lee adopted and essentially created for the movie, the heroic Chen Zhen, originally a real life student of Huo Yuanjia (about whom in reality, little is actually known).

Fist of Fury's enigmatic presentation of Chen Zhen has seen more sequels, reboots and adaptations celebrating the role Lee crafted than any of the other characters Lee portrayed. Whilst these various sequels, official: Jackie Chan in *New Fist of Fury* (1976), and otherwise, *Fist of Fury II* (1977), *Fist of Fury III* (1979) and *Fist of Legend* (1994).

TV adaptations – Donnie Yen's 1995 TV series of the same name, and re-interpretations – 2010's *Legend of the Fist* (Donnie Yen again), all vary in quality, none can really hold a candle to the original (with arguably the notable exception of Jet Li's *Fist of Legend*).

So why the enduring appeal? Why does the film manage to resonate in so many areas other than those we usually associate with its star? I would argue that it's because *Fist of Fury* is a movie that strives to be so much greater than the sum of its parts, far more so than the many of the other notable kung fu movies of the same era. It's part detective story, part love story, part melodrama and a very large part, an exceptional kung fu movie.

Yes, it has some spectacular martial arts action sequences, but then all of Bruce Lee's movies do, and most good Shaw Brothers kung fu movies certainly do. Bruce Lee was like a coiled spring onscreen, always poised to strike out with explosive, almost inhuman speed, but unlike many other martial arts actors of the era, Lee was every bit as watchable when he wasn't fighting as when he was and in this movie, that plays a very large part in the film's enduring appeal.

Fist of Fury more than any other of Lee's movies, crams in far more cinematic tropes into its relatively short run time than was common for most early '70s kung fu cinema. We get a truly multi-layered narrative, offering more than the standard revenge motivation so often seen in countless kung fu movies, yes there is an element of that here too, but here it's deftly wrapped up into an investigation, a mystery to be solved, much less 'you killed my master' and much more 'WHO killed my master and why?'

Lee's own investigation parallels the police's corrupt investigations into the trail of bodies that Chen Zhen leaves in his wake as he moves ever closer to the ringleader behind his beloved master's untimely death, and the closer he gets to the film's final reel, the more superhuman he becomes; few men of Lee's somewhat diminutive stature could lift a rickshaw and its passenger clean off the ground and toss it like a stick down the alley, but when Lee does just that, we somehow go with it, our hero is already transcending by that stage into something altogether more legendary. This element would be expanded upon even more in subsequent interpretations, never more so than by Donnie Yen in his 2010 film *Legend of the Fist – The Return of*

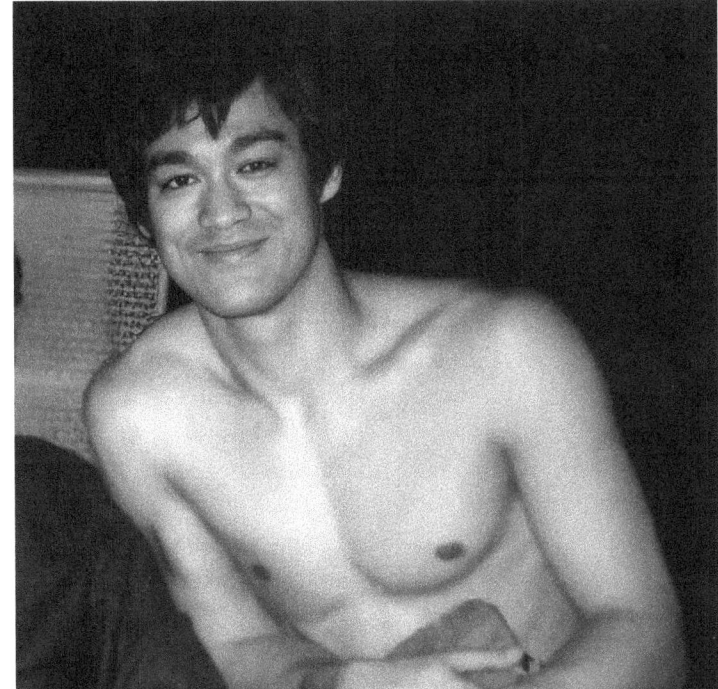

Chen Zhen in which Yen's Chen Zhen is basically Superman.

The movie also benefits significantly from Bruce Lee's massive respect and appreciation for Japanese Chanbara Cinema and the style of acting he had seen being displayed by its stars Toshiro Mifune and Tatsuya Nakodai; an acting style often defined by very large, almost over the top emotional displays, far larger than we would see on screen from Lee in his other roles. And for a movie which so vilifies its Japanese antagonists, it also borrows heavily from Japanese cinema in terms of styling, pacing and cinematography and it's all the better for it.

It's also one of the few early Golden Harvest productions that manages to almost rival the Shaw Brothers studio in terms of set design and construction. Suzuki's Garden Estate and the Japanese Dojo looking every bit as effective as some of the mammoth sets crafted at Shaws for Chang Cheh and Chor Yuen's larger budget outings.

It was years after I first saw this movie on BBC TV late at night in the UK, dubbed and missing all of its nunchuka sequences, to finally see the film uncut and in its original language. It's hard to go back to watch the dubbed version these days. I find it loses much of its impact and lots of its nuance, its dubbed dialogue having little of the charm of the Shaw Brothers movies' English dubs and making Lee's character sound far more like a monosyllabic Chinese John Wayne than the multi-layered character he was originally designed to be.

Lee's announcement when he first arrives to take on the Japanese students at their dojo that he is "the worst student of Jingwu" somehow manages to walk a line between being endearingly humble yet still confident enough in his own abilities to enter a massively outnumbered fight standing alone. The sequence that follows remains one of Lee's all time best and famously ends with Lee literally forcing the Japanese to 'eat their words' as he takes the banner left at his own school early on and feeds it back to his defeated opponents. The big rallying call to HK audiences that the smashing apart of this banner proclaiming the Chinese as 'The sick men of Asia' makes may go some way to explain the enormous success of the movie in HK, but it's maybe surprising to some that the film was,

and is still, immensely popular in Japan, despite their presence in the movie as the villains. The Japanese, always massive supporters of Bruce Lee's cinema, tend to have an eye for quality and for cinematic substance, both elements that *Fist of Fury* demonstrates in abundance. Like Run Run Shaw before him, Bruce Lee understood that Japanese cinema was (at that point in time), world leading in terms of its technique and execution. And he brought much of that same style to bear extremely effectively in *Fist of Fury*.

Fist of Fury Photographic Collection Vol. 1   35

Like the very best examples of enduring cinema from around the world, the film deals with universally human themes of grief, love, revenge and honour and handles them all with a skilful hand. It's very telling just how involved Lee was in the production when these same themes are so clumsily handled by director Lo Wei in some of his later movies, and indeed, the stories of Lee and Lo Wei's heated arguments on set are well documented. As too are the tales of Lee's rejection of the original short treatment for the movie and his demand for a more elaborate script to be produced (an act in itself very rare for HK cinema in the '70s and '80s).

The 'official' sequel *New Fist of Fury* starring Jackie Chan, also directed by Lo Wei, comes across as such a pale imitation of the original, whilst still dealing with much of the same themes, but with none of the nuance, grace and style that Lee infused into the original, that its hard to overstate Lee's influence on the production beyond his work in front of the camera.

We would also see several of the ideas on display here return in various forms in other Bruce Lee movies. We see the fantastic old man disguise he wears here make a return in *Game of Death* (though to me, in *Fist of Fury* they felt very much inspired by the original *Mission Impossible* TV series, Lee was a big fan of American TV and cinema too), and in *Game of Death* it was used by director Robert Clause to try to hide the fact that Bruce Lee was not present. In *Fist of Fury* I get a big kick out of the variety of different personas Lee as Chen Zhen adopts; the Jerry Lewis-style clown, the aforementioned frail old man, the telephone repair man, Lee manages to make us believe in each in turn.

Fist of Fury also presents us with Lee's only ever on-screen kiss, a short scene with the captivating Nora Miao, in an all too rare display of genuine affection frequently lacking from so much of HK's cinema. Action and otherwise.

Lastly, there is also the enduring legacy presented in the final shot of the movie, the freeze frame of our hero captured mid-flying kick to the sound of gunfire that serves not so much to signal his imminent demise but rather cementing him forever into cinema history; in much the same way as the climatic end shot of *Butch Cassidy and The Sundance Kid* does, we are spared seeing the hero's demise so the hero is effectively able to live on forever in our minds.

It's a movie I personally return to about once a year, usually in a double bill with Jet Li's *Fist of Legend*, sometimes in a triple feature with Wang Yu's *The Chinese Boxer*, which at times feels almost like a prototype for this movie, and in all honesty, *Fist of Fury* just gets better and better with every subsequent viewing. It remains, to this humble fan anyway… **Bruce Lee's greatest film.**

BRUCE LEE & NORA MIAO

Fist of Fury Photographic Collection Vol. 1

Fist of Fury Photographic Collection Vol. 1

MEMORIES OF FIST OF FURY
MICHAEL NESBITT

I don't have any memories of *Fist to Fury* when it was first released in the UK in July 1973, mainly due to the fact that I was only one month old at the time. However, by the time I became a fan of Bruce Lee in the mid-1980s, It didn't take me long to realize that *Fist of Fury* was one of the most important action films in the history of martial arts movies.

Way before social media and the Internet was a thing, the only way you could get information on your favorite action stars or martial arts movies, was through books or monthly magazines. Another way was through film, Betamax, or VHS. I remember so vividly as an awkwardly shy 13-year-old boy, asking my parents to get me a Bruce Lee video for my birthday. I had been so captivated by Bruce, as he was all the things I wasn't, strong, confident, and charismatic. His presence jumped out at you, and he was everything I wanted to be.

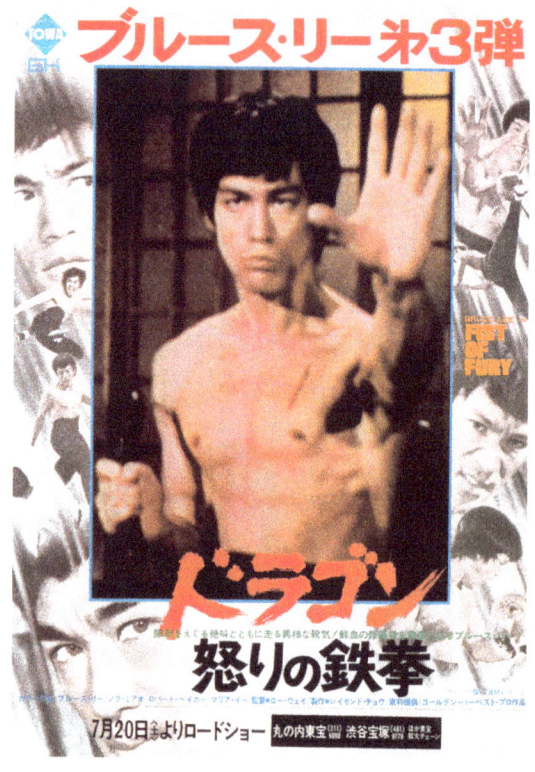

When my birthday finally came around, my parents agreed to get me the said video that I wanted, and when they asked me which one, I of course said *Enter the Dragon*. Unfortunately at the time, the video store didn't have it in stock, and the only Bruce Lee movie they did have was *Fist of Fury*. Slightly disheartened, carrying my newly acquired VHS in hand, I quickly scuttled back home to place it straight into our top-loading video player. The anticipation began taking hold of me, as I had only seen *The Big Boss* previously. Of course, it comes as no surprise that I sat there for the next hour and a half open-mouthed and in complete disbelief at the pure magnetism of Bruce as both an actor and martial arts film star. Even when I got to see *Enter the Dragon*, I still considered *Fist of Fury* to be the best martial arts movie I had ever seen.

One day, while I was reading an old magazine article on the BBFC (British Board of Film Classification) I was quite shocked to read that *Fist of Fury* had been cut. The famous

Fist of Fury Photographic Collection Vol. 1

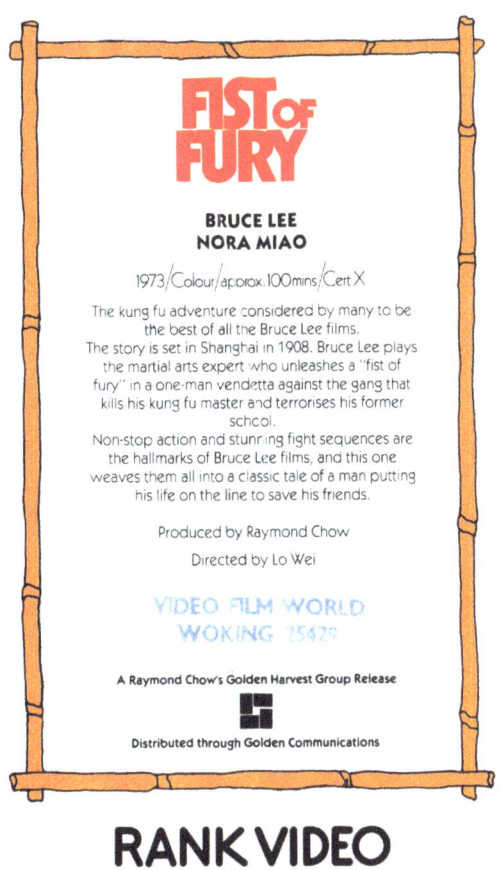

nunchaku scenes had been sliced out of the original movie. Even though I had seen many photos of Bruce using the nunchaku in *Fist of Fury*, it had never crossed my mind that the scene wasn't actually in it. As I carried on reading the article, it stated that the first release of *Fist of Fury*, the Rank version, wasn't cut, and it was only the later versions that had been butchered. A few months later, when I was browsing through the martial arts video section of the No 1 Video Store in Gateshead, there, sitting on the shelf right in front of me, was the first Rank Home Video release of *Fist to Fury*. You can imagine the excitement I felt at that moment, and I quickly grabbed it, took it to the counter, and hired it out for the day. As I got home and watched it, it was indeed the uncut version, and the cut scenes made the movie even better than it was before. I was so overwhelmed having this uncut version in my possession, that I decided to keep it. This was to be the first and only time I had stolen something. As the weeks went by, I thought I had gotten away with the most audacious robbery the north east of England had ever seen; however, that was about to change when my parents started receiving letters through the post from the No 1 Video Store.

Bob Baker hand signed autograph

Being only fourteen years old at the time, my parents didn't believe my innocent pleas, and they quickly found it when they searched my bedroom. Not only did I have to take it back, but they had to pay overdue fees, so it goes without saying that I received no pocket money for a long time, and was grounded for just as long.

The whole experience made me determined to get my very own uncut version of *Fist of Fury*, but I had to wait a couple of years for that to happen. When I was sixteen years old, I got myself a YTS job working in a warehouse, only making £28 a week. After I paid everything out, I was lucky to be left with a tenner. So I started saving. Back in those days, the late 1980s early 1990s, The only way you can get an uncut Chinese movie was through the black market or the underground scene. One such place was Shaolin Video, a mail-order company that sold hundreds of different Chinese martial arts movies, from Bruce Lee to Jackie Chan, from Shaw Brothers to Golden Harvest, they had them all, but they were expensive. At £28 a video + £2 postage, it was more than a week's wage for me, but I was determined to save enough money to make my first purchase. Three months went by, and I managed to save enough money to buy two VHS videos. One was the Bruce Lee Souvenir tape, which included the behind-the-scenes documentary *Enter the Dragon*, a few Bruce Lee trailers, and an episode of *The Green Hornet* on it. And the

48   *Fist of Fury* Photographic Collection Vol. 1

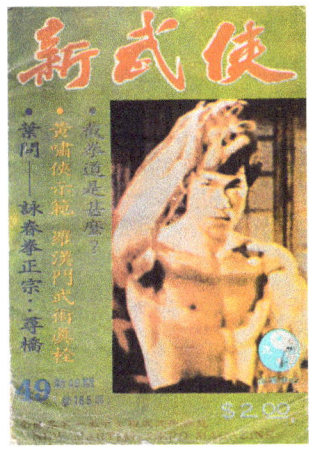   
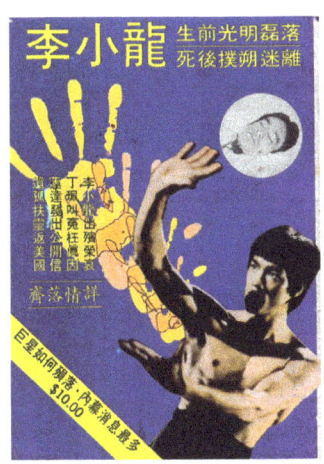   
  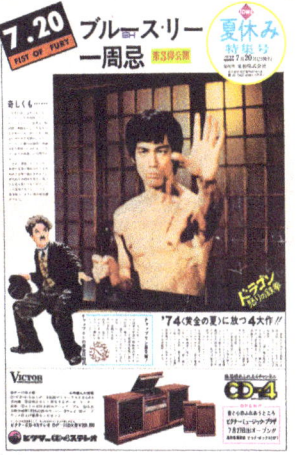 

second VHS video was of course the uncut version of *Fist of Fury*. When I received them through the post, I was more excited than I had ever been before. Finally, I had my very own copy of *Fist of Fury*, the best Bruce Lee movie of all time. God only knows how many times I watched it, and even though it was in Cantonese with no subtitles, it must have easily been over a hundred times. That was over thirty years ago now, and I still have the original VHS cover for it.

When I reminisce about my early years of being a Bruce Lee fan, my journey of finding and trying to own an uncut version of *Fist of Fury*, stands out as one of the best memories I have. I know many younger fans think that the movie is now dated, however, to me it's not only a part of history, more importantly, it's a part of my history.

RAYMOND CHOW Presents BRUCE LEE in FIST of FURY
Produced by Golden Harvest of Hong Kong, Directed by Lo Wei, also starring Nora Miao, James Tien, Maria Yi.

RAYMOND CHOW Presents BRUCE LEE in FIST of FURY
Produced by Golden Harvest of Hong Kong, Directed by Lo Wei, also starring Nora Miao, James Tien, Maria Yi.

GH RAYMOND CHOW Presents **BRUCE LEE in FIST of FURY**
Produced by Golden Harvest of Hong Kong, Directed by Lo Wei, also starring Nora Miao, James Tien, Maria Yi.

GH RAYMOND CHOW Presents **BRUCE LEE in FIST of FURY**
Produced by Golden Harvest of Hong Kong, Directed by Lo Wei, also starring Nora Miao, James Tien, Maria Yi.

RAYMOND CHOW Presents BRUCE LEE in FIST of FURY
Produced by Golden Harvest of Hong Kong, Directed by Lo Wei, also starring Nora Miao, James Tien, Maria Yi.

RAYMOND CHOW Presents BRUCE LEE in FIST of FURY
Produced by Golden Harvest of Hong Kong, Directed by Lo Wei, also starring Nora Miao, James Tien, Maria Yi.

GH RAYMOND CHOW Presents **BRUCE LEE in FIST of FURY**
Produced by Golden Harvest of Hong Kong, Directed by Lo Wei, also starring Nora Miao, James Tien, Maria Yi.

GH RAYMOND CHOW Presents **BRUCE LEE in FIST of FURY**
Produced by Golden Harvest of Hong Kong, Directed by Lo Wei, also starring Nora Miao, James Tien, Maria Yi.

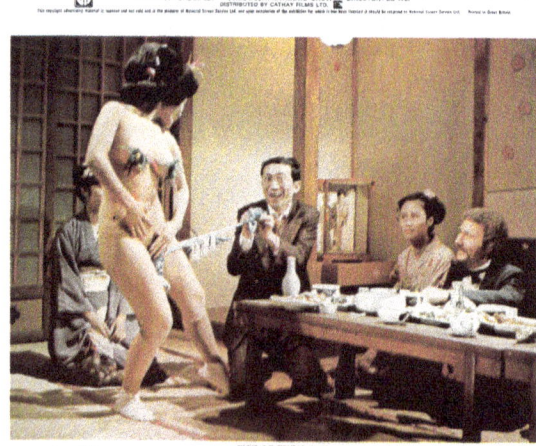

Fist of Fury Photographic Collection Vol. 1

CHINESE NOT ALLOWED

THE GERMAN CONNECTION
THOMAS GROSS

Thomas has one of the best collections of Posters and Lobby cards I have seen in Europe. I was grateful that he took the time out to scan and share some of his *Fist of Fury* memorabilia items that he had acquired over the years to present in this special *FOF* edition.

THOMAS: I was born in 1962 and started collecting Bruce Lee items in 1975. My first item was the German *Kung Fu Monthly* poster magazine. I collected all of the German martial arts magazines in which I could find reports about Bruce Lee. In 1978 the last Bruce Lee film *Game of Death* (German title: *Mein Letzter Kampf*) came out in Germany. With this new Bruce Lee euphoria many new items were published and produced by the German film distributor Scotia Film and a German dealer Budo Artikel Herbert Velte. Of course, the magazines and posters produced in Hong Kong were also sold by the Bruce Lee Jeet Kune Do Club.

Let's move on to *Fist of Fury* now (German title: *Todesgrüsse Aus Sanghai*). The film premiered in Germany on June 28, 1973, just a few weeks before Bruce Lee's death. Unfortunately, I wasn't old enough to see the film in the cinema back then. I had to wait until 1978 when Bruce Lee's films were re-released. But I was definitely very impressed by this film, especially the nunchaku scenes. After watching the film everyone made these nunchucks out of regular broomsticks and practiced trying to be as good as Bruce Lee. I had a lot of bruises at that time. At about the same time you could finally take Bruce Lee's films back home with you, you could buy the first Super 8 films. From 1980 the first video tapes came out and since then I have collected many articles and lots of other items and of course I am particularly proud of them.

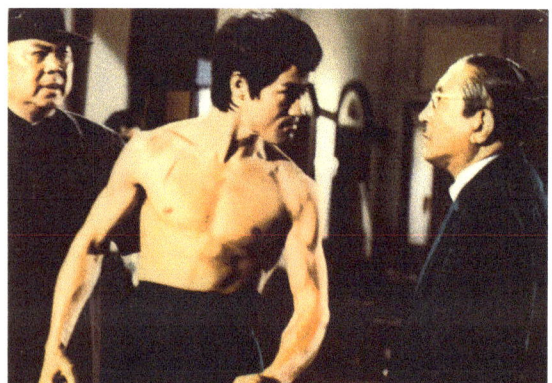

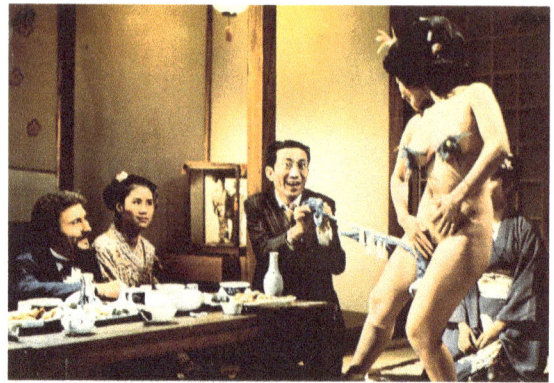

Todesgrüsse aus Shanghai

Todesgrüsse aus Shanghai

Todesgrüsse aus Shanghai

Todesgrüsse aus Shanghai

FILMWAYS
AUSTRALASIAN DISTRIBUTORS PTY. LTD.
EXHIBITOR'S PRESS SHEET

SYNOPSIS

In 1908 Chen arrives in Shanghai to attend the funeral of his teacher Ho, founder of the Famous School of Chinese Martial Arts. During his visit the rival Japanese Arts Association insult the Chinese people and single handed, he attacks the Japanese Association.

The Headmaster of the Japanese Association demands that Chen be handed over to him for punishment. While trying to escape Chen discovers his Teacher had in fact been murdered and suspects the Japanese. During the fight to capture him, and his efforts to prove the guilt of the Japanese Association he kills their Headmaster, fights and kills their best students

Chen of murdering the Japanese Headmaster. Chen makes a hasty escape. He then appears on the roof of the school and the film comes to a startling climax.

International cast of Europe's top Kung Fu Experts.

CREDITS

Directed and Written by
BRUCE LEE

ACCESSORIES

DAYBILLS
SLIDES
PRESS SHEETS
TRAILERS

RUNNING TIME 103 min.

LENGTH 2826 m.

including a famed Russian exponent of the martial arts.

Satisfied this is revenge enough Chen decides to leave Shanghai he then finds that all his old school friends have been mysteriously massacred. While planning his next action the Japanese Consul arrives with the Chief of Police and accuses

BRUCE LEE CONFRONTATIONS

Fist of Fury Photographic Collection Vol. 1

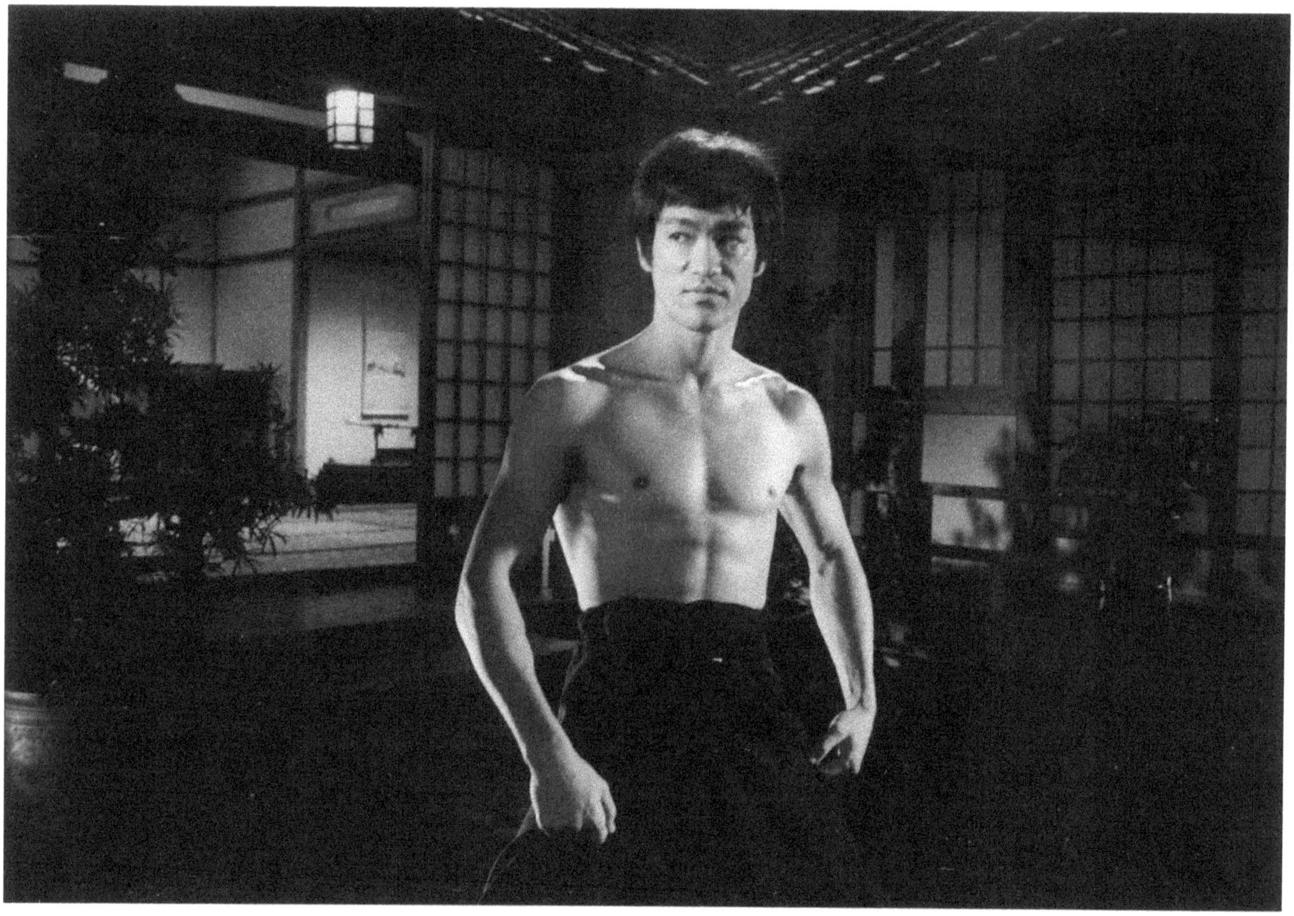

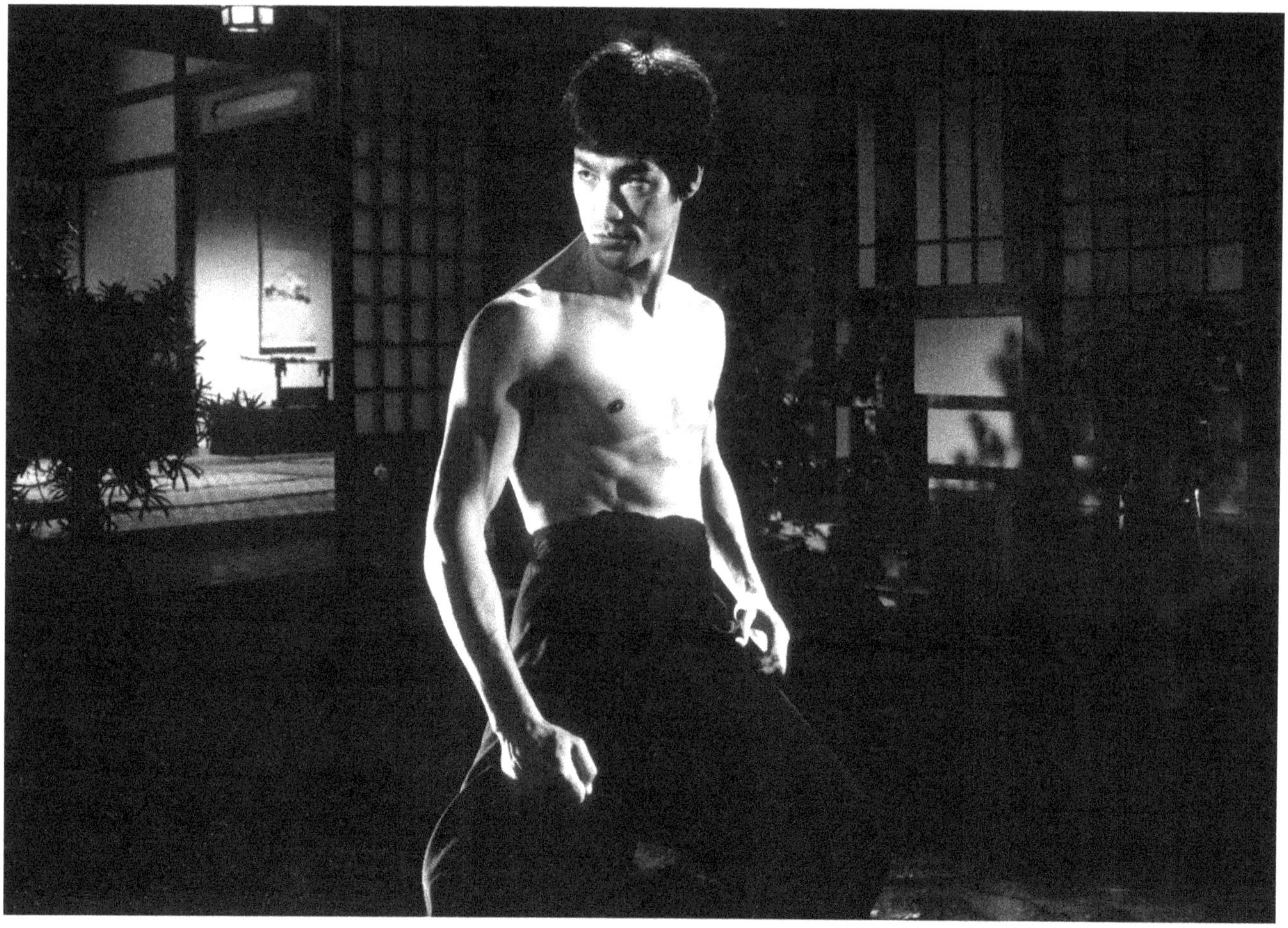

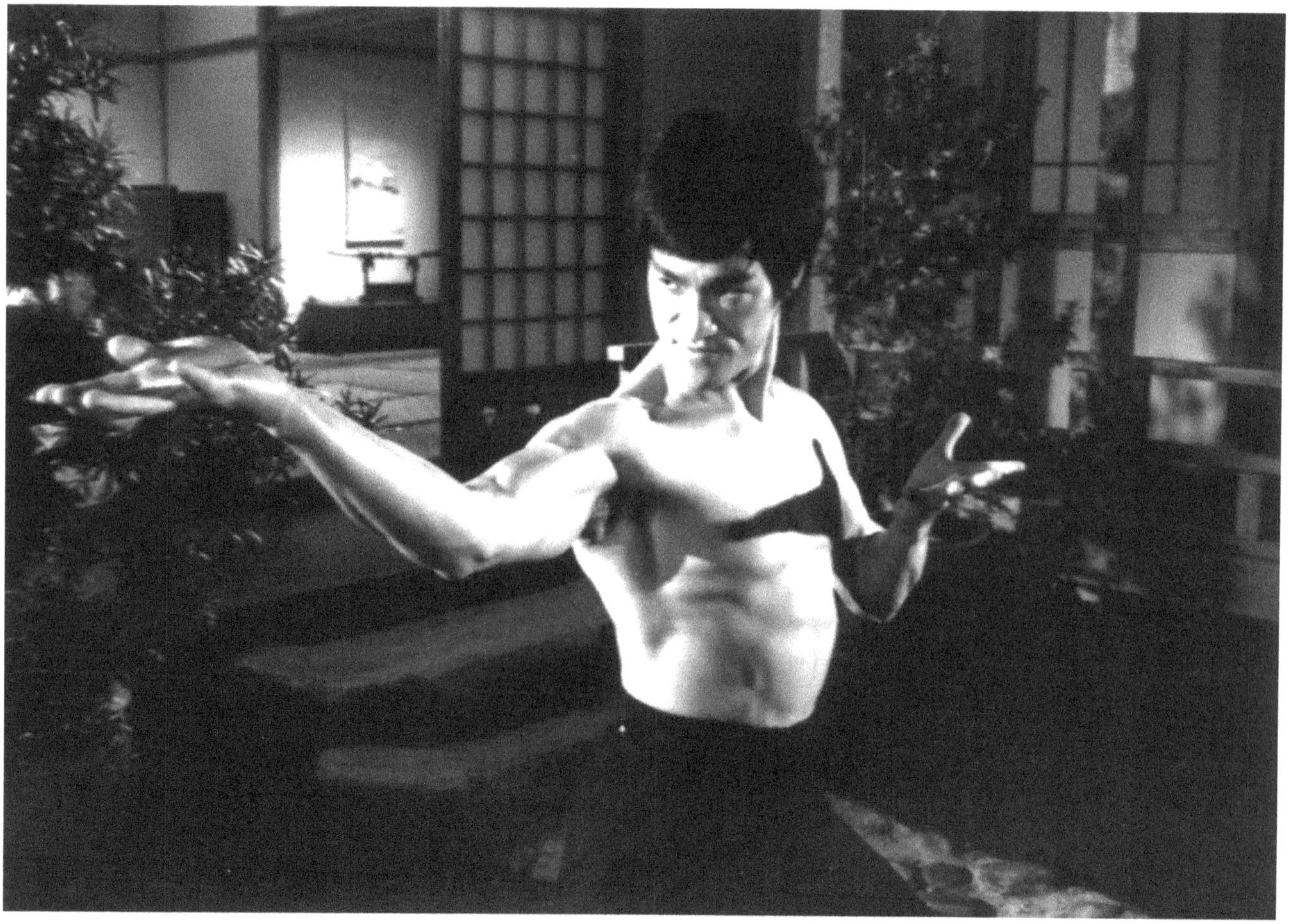

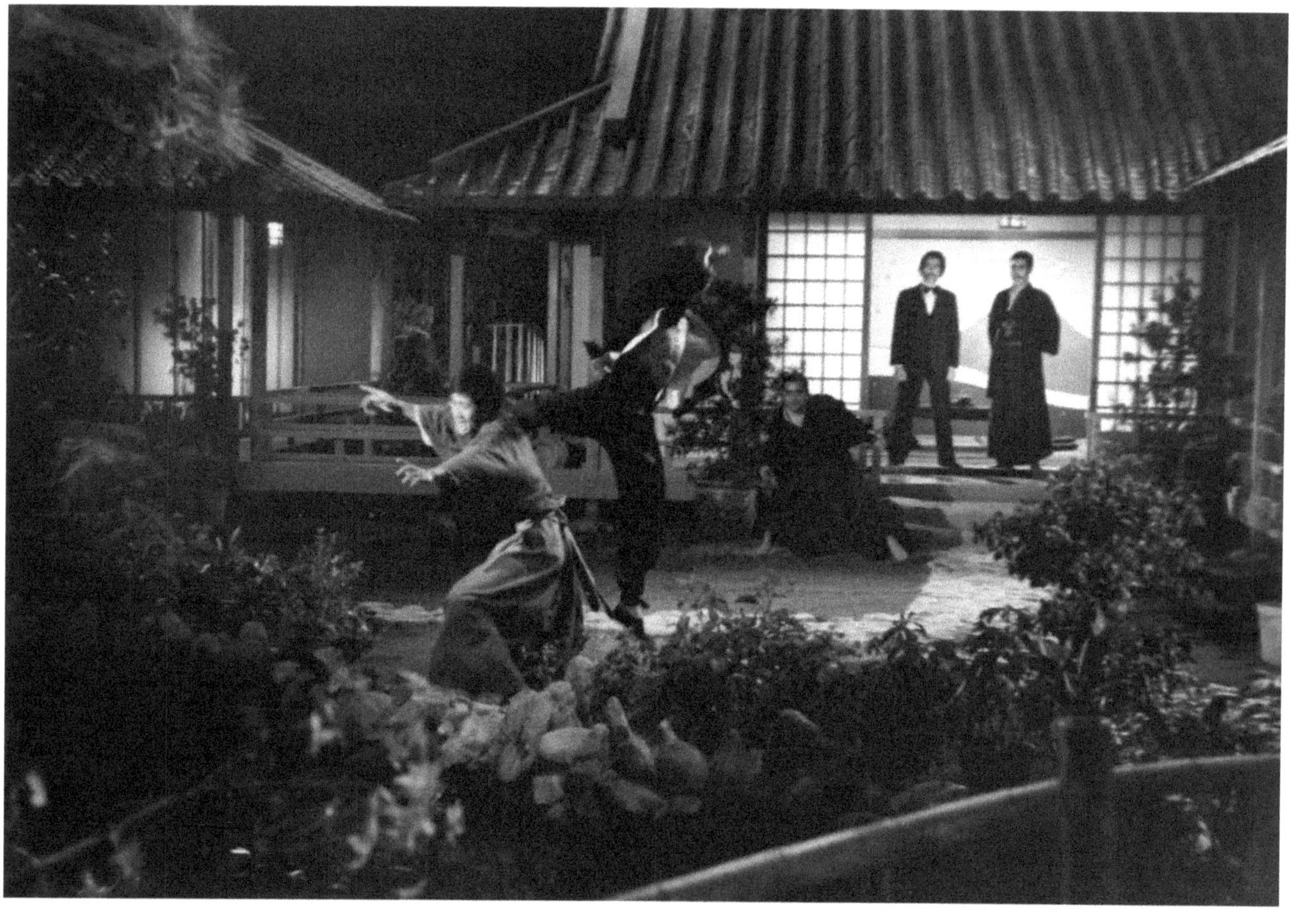

84   *Fist of Fury* Photographic Collection Vol. 1

Fist of Fury Photographic Collection Vol. 1

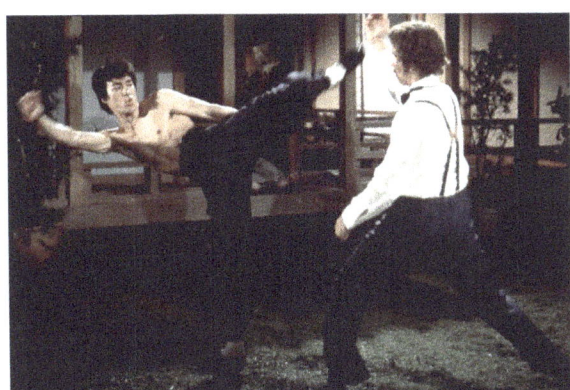

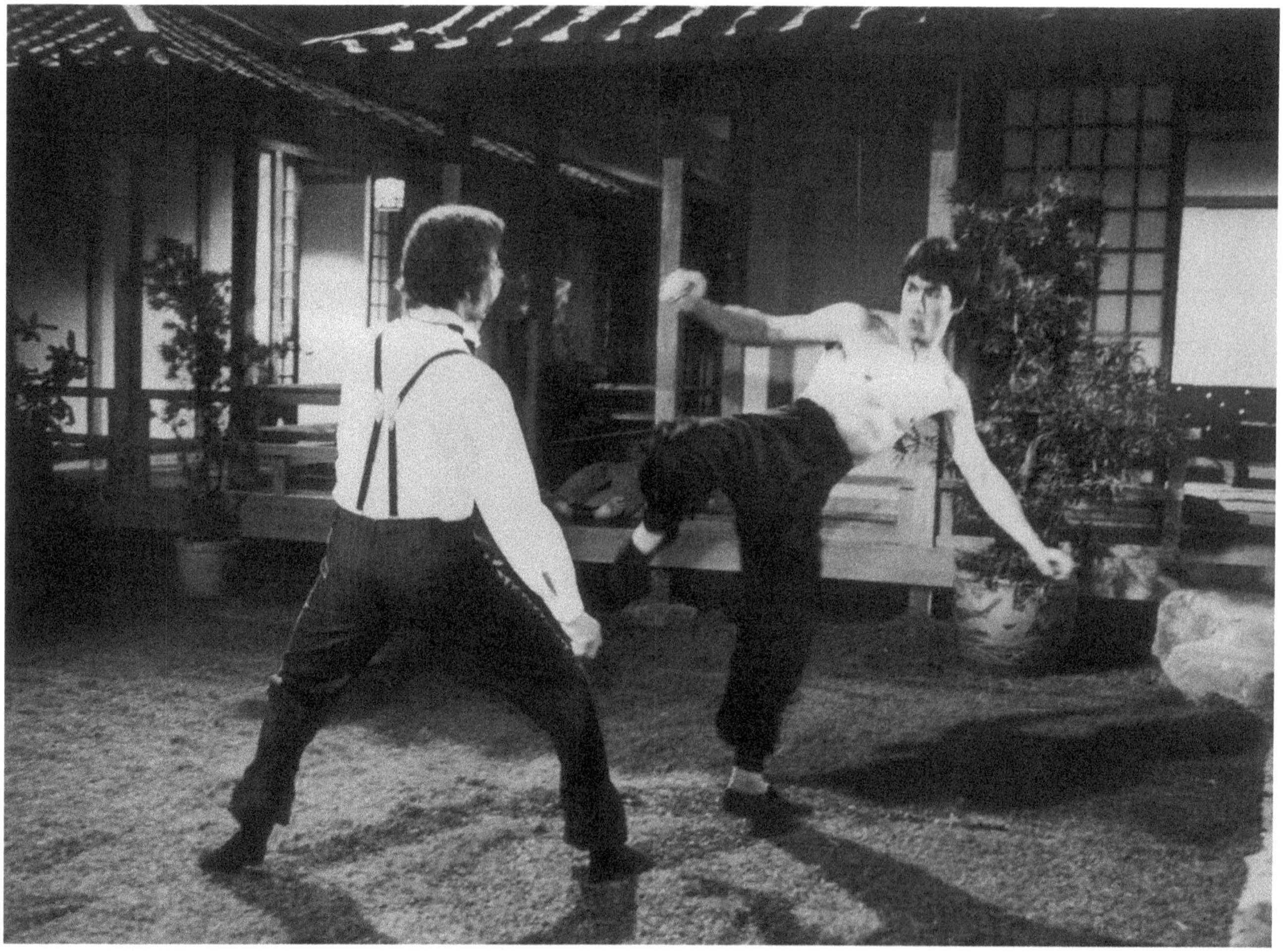

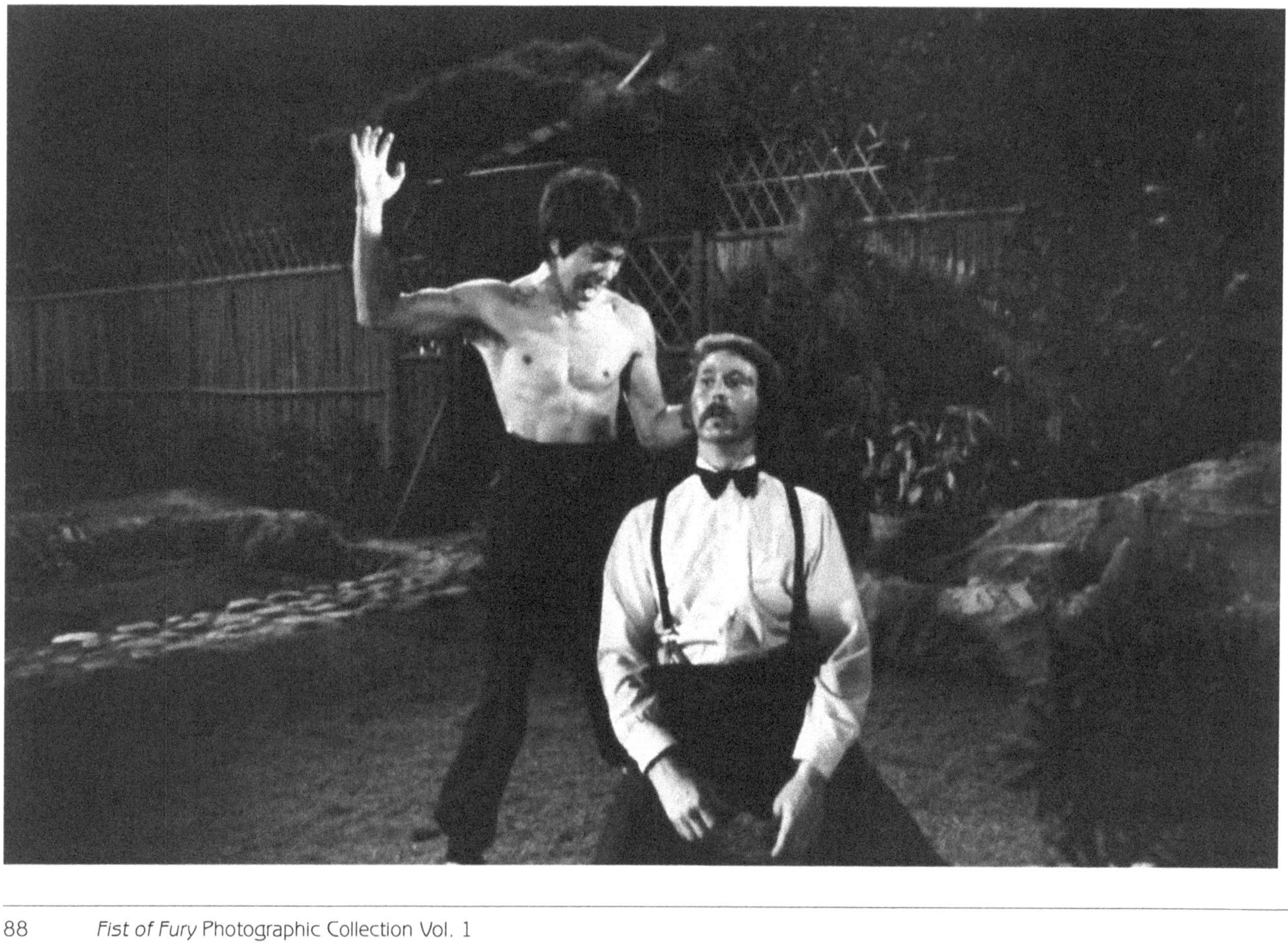

Fist of Fury Photographic Collection Vol. 1

MORE MEMORIES OF FIST OF FURY
JAMES McKEON

First and foremost, I will introduce myself. My name is James McKeown. I have been a Bruce Lee aficionado since 1974, when I was eleven years old. Back then, seeing a Bruce Lee film at my local cinema was an epic task, requiring great ingenuity and military-grade planning. I have vivid memories of being determined to get past the age barrier that hindered my enjoyment of this new, exciting superstar. Trying to get into an 18 as a pre-teen was no easy feat! Luckily, I did have a family friend at one cinema who told me that if I did get in, to just sit at the back and don't talk to anyone.

Thinking back, some of the schemes we came up with were crazy! It's a shared experience for many of us old school Bruce fans, who recall our slightly embarrassed memories with good humour! How on earth did I contrive to add seven years onto my actual age? Well, I tried the old trick of sticking tea leaves under my nose, of course. Or I'd try to draw a moustache onto my upper lip. I've heard so many stories about aborted and disastrous attempts! The classic would be kids who were unable to give their (fake) correct date of birth to the ticket booth staff. They mustn't have thought that far ahead! Man, I've so many classic 'wrong date of birth' stories.

Some prototype spies would fail spectacularly at the first hurdle in other ways. The best one I heard was when the ticket clerk asked a kid whether he wanted a half or full ticket. Guess what they said? Yep, a half! What they ended up receiving was a one-way ticket to getting booted out! Some of the cinema staff seemed to revel in a good 'gotcha' moment. The teal eaves strategy wasn't a guarantee of success, because sometimes they fell off, and the ticket clerk would take one look at you and just laugh, telling you to come back in ten years.

That was when you'd try another cinema showing a Bruce Lee film. You'd stand by the exit, waiting for someone to leave. If you were cunning enough, bingo! You could sneak in successfully. Yes, those moments were the destinies of youthful Bruce Lee fans back in the '70s.

Fist of Fury Photographic Collection Vol. 1

Enter the Dragon was the first Bruce film I saw, at the tender age of eleven, followed by *Fist of Fury*. Obviously, in the UK we didn't see *Way of the Dragon* until after his passing (though it was shown in Chinatown cinemas in '72/'73, if you knew the 'when' and the 'where'). Bruce has been lost six months prior to the showings I saw, sadly, but the effect was still the same. I had never seen any action actor that possessed those skills, delivered with such speed and grace.

In Blackpool, we had many cinemas: the Pavillion, the Regent, the Odeon, the ABC, the Palladium, and more. The flicks and the flea pit were just a couple of the names we called them. Sadly, they are all bingo halls or whatever today. The time of every town having a dozen picture houses are gone.

After seeing *Enter the Dragon*, *Fist of Fury* continued to wow me. Enjoying Bruce's animal instincts and war cries again was magical. The story, as all fans will know, concerns Japanese occupation. After villains kill his teacher, Chen (Bruce) enters DEFCON 1 revenge mode, killing or maiming anything or anyone who stands in his way. I recall that occasionally the film was shown with another Bruce flick (*The Big Boss* or *Enter the Dragon*), but not always. Sometimes the double bill was populated by *Fist of Fury* and a non-Bruce movie. And it was known for that other film to be a dodgy sex movie! In such cases, it was best to keep close to the exit doors! They were very strange times. I won't say any more on that, but old school fans know what I'm talking about! Getting back to *Fist of Fury*, I have a great memory of a fellow patron shouting, "Count them, you [swear word]!" about the punches during the Bruce Lee/Bob Baker fight. I gotta say, I laughed uncontrollably!

I must say that *Fist of Fury* is probably the best Bruce film in terms of storyline. The Chinese were described as "the sick men of Asia", but Bruce's performance firmly laid this attitude to rest. He became huge in Hong Kong, and even in Japan. That's a strange twist, isn't it? He spends the whole film, from beginning to end, beating the Japanese down, but in real life he's like a god to them! It's a great film. Annoyingly, in the UK it suffered cuts and poor editing, but that's just how it was back then. No nunchakus? No end flying kick? Pathetic. But we just had put up with it. The BBFC had got there before us.

Nevertheless, what a privilege to watch the films of the Little Dragon at the time of release. The cinemas of the past are long forgotten, but memories of them are cherished. It's expensive to go cinema today. Even the popcorn and drinks are daylight robbery. However, for the older crowd, there's a beacon of nostalgia. In 2016, The Regent reopened in my town, Blackpool. Its focus is on the experience of the moviegoers of yesteryear. It's not

open as I write, due to Covid, but hopefully it will return in good health, so people like myself can recapture the magic of going to the flicks in the '70s.

I continued to go to the cinema to watch Bruce films as often as possible in my youth and actually made it to legitimate showings at the age of eighteen, lol. I must admit that I probably can't remember every visit, but at a guess I watched the films hundreds of times at various cinemas. I even walked to Fleetwood to watch his movies if they weren't showing in Blackpool, or jumped on the tram. Many times I stayed to watch the repeated showings. It saved paying twice or three times! Great memories. I look back at these times with great fondness. Being a Bruce Lee fan isn't dull. I am fifty-eight now, and my years haven't changed me. I still find the Dragon to be my greatest inspiration. He was, and still is, a unique actor and martial artist.

The passage of time has continued to fire the sparks of excitement. Years after watching *Fist of Fury* at the cinema, it was eventually made available on VHS. The Rank Video release in the '80s, procured from a video rental shop, was actually circulated (in error IMHO) uncut. What a welcome surprise! Yes! Finally a chance to see Bruce's movie exactly as it was meant to be! It's a classic film and still stands the test of time.

Over the decades I have collected anything and everything related to Bruce Lee. I have several pieces of autographed material from *Fist of Fury*, seen in these images. I also have great memories of sneaking into movie showings as a schoolboy! I hope my small story brings memories flooding back for other old school peeps like me. Enjoy them! I have a group on Facebook for selling and trading, or just talking about anything Bruce Lee-related. Feel free to join. Thanks for reading and keep the faith!

MODELS OF FURY
GLYNN DARBYSHIRE

Glynn kindly sent me a selection of stunning photographs from his private collection showcasing some of the excellent action figures from Bruce Lee's *Fist of Fury*.